running with *light*

Also by Luke Davies

Four Plots for Magnets (1983)
Absolute Event Horizon (1995)
Candy (1997)

poems by

luke davies
running
with *light*

Allen & Unwin

First published in 1999 by
Allen & Unwin
9 Atchison Street
St Leonards NSW 1590 Australia
Phone: (61 2) 8425 0100
Fax: (61 2) 9906 2218
E-mail: frontdesk@allen-unwin.com.au
Web: http://www.allen-unwin.com.au

National Library of Australia
Cataloguing-in-Publication entry:

Davies, Luke, 1962– .
  Running with light: poems.

  ISBN 1 86508 012 8.

  I. Title.

A821.3

Set in 11/18 pt New Caledonia by Bookhouse Digital, Sydney

10 9 8 7 6 5 4 3 2 1

for Mum and Dad

Contents

PART ONE: *Pulse*

PART TWO: *Still Life*

Part One: PULSE

Dew   3

Diving the *Coolidge*   7

Passage of Time   11

Wave Function, Bondi   15

Sea Shanty II   17

Love and Death   21

Pollen   23

Birth of Venus   25

Fortune of the Shipwrecked   27

Safety of Descent   29

Flowers   31

Winter   33

Ezekiel   35

Rain   37

Small Spaces   39

Wind   41

Summer   43

Blood   45

Fish   47

The Bridges of Paris   49

The Lavender Minutes   51

Rue des Abbesses   53

Excavation   55

Airmail   59

Four Postcards   65

Crescent Moon Over the Eiffel Tower   69

Lisbon   71

Part Two: STILL LIFE

Weather   75
The Veins of Howard Hughes   77
Premonition of Her Disappearance from the Life   79
Miscarriage   81
History of Violence   83
Childhood Terror   85
Bodies of Water   87
The Persistence of Loss   89
History of Real Estate   91
Prayer in May   93
From Theory to Pulse   95

Notes   97
Acknowledgements   101

Think back to Einstein's first thought experiment— running with light. What the second and first postulates imply is that not only can you never catch up to a light wave, but you can't even get close... Referenced to nothing (that is, without an ether), the speed of light is unvarying. If something comparable existed in spatial terms, it would have the property that no matter where you went, it was always the same distance away from you. You could get neither closer to it, nor farther away from it; the separation would be fixed. This is what infinity is like. No matter how far toward it or away from it one travels, it remains the same infinite distance away. As Einstein said, the speed of light plays the role of an infinitely great velocity. Light has no place, but it does have a speed and we are always separated from it by 299,792,458 metres per second.

> —Arthur Zajonc, *Catching the Light:*
> *the Entwined History of Light and Mind*

Part One
PULSE

Dew

Years ago, the pioneering geophysicist Teddy Bullard
told me that trying to understand the structure of the
Earth by analyzing earthquakes was like trying to
understand the structure of a grand piano by listening
to the noise it made when pushed down a staircase.
Ever since, I have been fascinated by the subject.
—John Gribbin

The huge earth, bigger than we can
possibly imagine, held together as if by
string or magic. The huge earth smelling
of jasmine and honeycomb, poppy dust
and diesel, everything forever speeding
over the glacial horizon towards
our saturated nostrils, to the middle
of the moment and the tropical fact
of the blood's beat, now. The huge earth
a quarter of the age of the universe.
Earth. Late at night in the silence
we can hear the rumble and clack
of its almost impossible orbit

through the solar system. It strains
to shatter circumference. And we
mistake such ferocity for the distant
noise of industry. But the sun
gathers its planets and all of us
hurtle through the spiral fringes
of the galaxy, out here where distance
is so great that hurtle can seem entirely
the wrong word. Rumble then. Rumble
through the fringes. The galaxy itself
in desolate serenity ploughing across
light years of emptiness light years
from anywhere. Nothing but neutrinos
there: massless and silent they stream
through us, through the vast empty spaces
in our molecules. Nothing but photons,
raining light through space to us
so the universe unfolds upon our eyes
like the Cinema of Brutal Grace exploding
frame by frame. Pop Pop. A great
unassessable beauty. This can be
too much or everything you've ever
desired. And because only what is
containable is infinite (or infinitely
memorable) we reel it in, from space

to local spaces. The huge earth shudders.
The old rocks groan and a black wind howls
but in the cracks it is possible to feel
nothing but stillness. At Foxground
stillness in the hour before dawn, as if
we were all there is. The mist hung
like a hammock across the valley
and swayed in the thick yellow rays
of the moon. The horse emerged
from shadow, snorted, stamped twice,
desiring to break the monolithic
silence. Ah noise, night, ground. Our feet
and her hooves. The moon like a message,
'You are here.' In light resides memory,
in sound the great grind of the stones
of the earth, hauling their sad souls
through the dark tectonic heat. Such
easy power in the rocks and in the air,
welling up and bearing down and us
in-between. Joy in the shock of the dew
on the soles of our feet in the knife-
edge of dawn. In the blood's beat peace.

Diving the *Coolidge*

I

The more you dive the more dreams come.
On the island of Espiritu Santo
the ghosts of Spaniards drift in the heavy heat
of a copra breeze, four hundred years old
those ghosts. The *S.S. President Coolidge*
is a living force, a great dream factory
under the water: suddenly you submerge
and a world opens out slow and cool
and implacable. You glide through jeeps,
cranes, ballrooms, a barbershop. You are falling
down the promenade deck, which once
lay level with the gold horizon. Once, in 1933,
a couple kissed here, maybe 1934. Once it was
a luxury liner, then a troop carrier, now
it looms a palace of shadow and curve distorted
by the wordless press of atmospheres. An angel fish
hovers on the edge of vision always there
motionless and every direction is up
and light a distant thing like memory.

A seahorse nibbles on a chandelier.
The ocean dreams, you seem to dream in it.

II

Between dives you read about Daniel Boone.
How once in Kentucky he camped by a creek
in the middle of nowhere, and dreamed.
Deep dreams, strong dreams, unusual for Boone,
who slept with an ear to the smallest noise.
Water unfurling the geometry of fragmentation,
which is consciousness, or the way a stick snaps
and you are not wholly dissolved.
Boone wakes and says, 'I call this Dreaming Creek.'

The sparkle of water clacking on pebbles.
Sunlight like a secret in Kentucky,
flooding the glade and the tiny rapids.

Between and during dives it becomes apparent
that if land is an enclosure of order and light
surrounded by the formlessness of ocean

then Dreaming Creek in Kentucky
—the specific named after the nebulous—
is a small slit in the world, a pathway
from daylight to water, from Daniel Boone
to Espiritu Santo, in the great ocean,
where the more you dive the more dreams come.
The ocean dreams, you seem to dream in it.

Boone sleeping and the water gurgling.
At forty metres your dreams meet his.
Dream sunlight like a secret in Kentucky.

III

You are diving a giant dream called the *Coolidge*
and the more you dive the more dreams come.
You feel you could fall forever, towards
the gathering dark. The thick blue of descent.
In the smoking room, above the fireplace,
you come across a lady and a unicorn
and run your hands along them
where the seaweed sways on their porcelain flesh.

The dark sea all around you filled with flakes,
the statue large through goggles in that gloom.

That night you dream the lady alive:
she is Anastasia, pale and waiflike junkie
you barely knew, Anastasia with nothing,
not even hope, who drank arsenic
seven years ago, who you never think of.
She comes to you in her Elizabethan finery
on a wide windy beach with her unicorn,
and the *Coolidge* refloats and you wear
the Captain's hat. The way dreams work.

You on the bridge gleaming with pride.
Anastasia dead these years and arsenic
a kind of drowning. Seaweed swaying
on her hard white skin. I remember
everything. I remember I felt
nothing. In dream begins compassion.

Passage of Time

The mules that angels ride come slowly down
The blazing passes, from beyond the sun.
   —Wallace Stevens, 'Le Monocle de Mon Oncle'

I

The humility of long journeys. God
may it be mine. Nothing may make sense
but it comes as no surprise
that neutrinos pour through everything, through dense

matter and nothing at all. They rain
everywhere and all the time and in our blood
we sense this. Photons, too, stream
to us in an unassuming flood

of light, though if we're not here
to see them, there is no light.
The eye like a light-sponge, but hard
and metallic, popping the photon in flight.

II

The hawk has no complexity
but what it knows of joy is in its eye
and wells up in its wings—its huge heart
sending pulses through the sky

over the plains near Coonabarabran,
where my father went one day.
Dad the Ranger. Sadness. His love
and all the things he couldn't say.

He scales the rocks to the nest, knowing
the world is mostly full of what's undone.
Like everyone, he wants to be that hawk.
But some call it freedom; he calls it sin.

And does he know peace? I do not know.
As he tags the chicks, a kind of content.
From the high crag he spies the hawk
in flight. Sadness. Not *his* element.

III

The humility of journeys. The great
grace of moving. On a brittle
day through the pulsing air dived the hawk,
preposterously handsome and a little

evil and desirable and then we are desirous
of all things. In the journey through blood, to see
that eye and through that eye,
to be a father and to be

a son, before the show
wraps up. Just once. The weight
of all that past and all that dust—
we are landbound, have not the might

to meet in the cold hard air
nor the strength to devour the rat
scurrying on the baked earth between us.
Always the rat between us and great rest.

Always the dark shadow of a greater hawk
looming above us and blocking the sky:
oh father with your sparrow bones, death
descends on you and that's your day.

Wave Function, Bondi

In the odd world of the quantum, things
appear to exist in a multitude of states—
describable only as the set of probabilities
known as a wave function—until tipped
into a definite outcome by an act of
'measurement.'

— John McCrone

I am floating or falling. I am light
as a feather, or even my thumbprint

fills the sky. The water near shore
shines silver on a cold Spring day.

A helicopter punctuates the air
and I imagine, further out, there are fish

drifting mindlessly in subtle currents
deeper than green goes. Fish made from atoms

streamed and condensed to the hard steel bliss
of shape; fish

of whose precise location
I am dreamily uncertain.

I imagine the bends: how pain swoops
to painlessness the way smack takes you

away from yourself—vertigo. I feel bubbles
of nitrogen fizz distantly in my cool toes.

I imagine fins, or changes in current
surmised, in the dark, as fins.

Yet the heat in my head and the light
on my eyes are the same blue day's

convergence. This is the limitless
space between horizons.

Sea Shanty II

Everyone gets kicked and the cabin-boy
kicks the cat—motto for living,
a decade all at sea. Beware

of the Chathams! Beware
of the Chathams! (the engine room pumping
like a desperate heart);

and hard alee, awash, you'd sail on
regardless, again and again
to the hull-splitting reefs.

Ah the bags of go and bags of guts,
the wholly demented faith
of the rudderless voyage—

how does a boat limp?
From the Chathams you'd limp into land
by the skin of a whisker guy.

Anyway swapping ports meant only
a black dog for a white monkey.
April Fool torpedoes, nothing there

but the mocking phosphorescence
of events just missed.
Give me some time to blow myself down:

even becalmed, your very breath carried
the deep lassitude of shipwreck.
Kelp stench in the doldrums

or the gale force hissing of fear,
same day forever on the endless sea,
same fudging of the captain's log.

These parts be inhabited by dragons:
then SatNav comes and clears the maps
of all that dark unease. Sun or moon,

the ocean is an ocean then,
the sky a tidal pulse of light
ridden like a wave by satellites

whose power is greater than my own
dead reckoning. Minesweeper's prayer:
from things that go bump in the night,

deliver us.

Love and Death

She is the light in the bay, the guide.
She is the angel and holy object. Sings
her empty garments into the billowing
of her, the fullness of her form and self.
She is the motion that circles make.

She is not mine. The water of the bay
drops green and deep. There were times she said,
'We must go shopping,' and I thought it was
magic I heard. Walls tumbled at her breath.
The holiest city in India. God.

You lick that rose and waves come on.
She is at ease beyond ideas
where earthquakes form in the ocean's floor.
Muscles tighten and she shudders once and
she blends with the cool air sighing.

The myth of love! I know her, separate;
she's in the world. But all we know is blood.

The bay's on fire, the beach is soaked in red.
You try to imagine that she is opaque
like an angel who floods you with blue

in the night: but staring at the palms, it's just
the appalling darkness of the waves you see
and the darkness you hear
                              of their crashing.

Pollen

The tulips open from an Alpine girl. You are on
the pollen path, and the smell of pollen is in her,
and you are kissing her, her mouth is open.

You are on the pollen path and the tulips,
bathed in sunlight, accentuate the obvious,
that the path is only one of many but still it is

the path. It begins invisibly, here in the arms
of the Alpine girl, gold hair and the golden
dust of midday, she is stroking you, you

are stroking her, you are kissing her, her
mouth is hot. When she hits the trance
she is still the Alpine girl but somehow also

not, and the sun is everywhere and the room too
fills with pollen. She is kissing your neck, itself
a kind of stem, her tongue the hummingbird,

the room a field of breezes and carressings.
In the trance where tulips sway, her legs
reach to the sky, the air heats, the atmosphere

billows. The unified field, in the time of pollen,
in the radiant heat, everything leaving and entering
in flood: *your hands are pollen, your body is pollen.*

Wave is amplified and particle is amplified
but in the heart of the flower, in the budding,
in the nectar, in the stamen, we sense them as one

and your eyes are pollen and your kiss is pollen.

Birth of Venus

—for K.B.

Lay yourself down you are
breathed upon the beach you are
sighed by the water and the wind

In your eyes the ocean
the way love works
the big in the little thing

Fortune of the Shipwrecked

In your eyes the ocean.
I have lied my way through every

situation. To hustle was to be pure.
But the soul of the water:

I am washed ashore, marinely led.
I bathe in the light

of the star of untruth
which is shining on the midnight kelp.

The star of untruth: the irony.
My matted hair and the purple bruises.

My own wrung soul on the briny shore
where the soul of the water laps

like a whisper of Spring.
In your eyes the ocean.

The infinite sadness of finite joys
in the season of rain and death

when the magpies sing.

Safety of Descent

Miranda Miranda come see all
the tiny new worlds:

then I saw her face,
now I'm a believer.

If tomorrow the world
turned upside down

we would slowly adjust
to watching TV. Perhaps.

Or look before diving,
for fear of the air.

There is nothing to fear
in the vault of the air

or the earth's deep vaults.
The termite builds a house of holes

but all I see
is the sea in your eyes.

By Babylon we wept into the stream
your holy tears, forgetfulness.

The earth decays. The water was,
is now and ever shall be.

You are good like the moon
and the moon rules the tides.

Flowers

Lark and rose go mad, even with winter
coming on, the garden beneath the verandah blooms,
the park is dense with sun and soccer balls.
By lark I mean generic bird, God knows
the names for all these things with wings. Ditto
the rose: the garden drooling colour and bloom.
Lavender I recognise, and jasmine climbing
the concrete wall, and a real rose in the corner,

red as blood. I meant to say: birds and flowers
go ballistic, even with winter coming on.
Carrying on their own life. The earth drowns
in the blooming. Even when there is no wind there is
the solar wind, whipping our bodies from the depths of space.
Ferocities of trees bent double. Playing soccer,
nobody notices this. The far park flutters in mirage.
The jasmine is awash with butterflies.

Winter

The bees come here. Their fatness is a blessing.
Weighed down by the salt in the air but enlightened
by nectar, they fly, but only just, but wearily.
At times of the year, that will do. There is no bee
beyond that here who drowns in the stamen of the sea holly
and drowns again tomorrow, all bees the one bee.
There is no high verandah save for this.
There is the sun, and bees weighed down by light.

Down there the salt haze billows from the waves
and spreads across the bowl the suburb makes,
as if the sea were cane fields all aflame,
upwind, and sugar filled the sky, and smoke.
Down there the dead bees line the high tide line.
Up here the honey myrtle, star jasmine, zephyr, and sun.
Garden as cynosure of pollen and treacle; lushness of winter
when hearts are thin; juice unbrittling the brittle air.

Ezekiel

I see the massive weather change all day
and feel the planet swing through space: oxygen
a reprieve, atmosphere the illusion of a comfort zone.
Outside the wheel the going gets tough, because
it is raw, and you are not alive, could never be.
Open the pod bay door, HAL. On earth the birds
twitter, their tiny lungs work overtime. It seems
a shallow panting place. And then the bee,

which is abundance, with its fat belly, drones
into my life. Meaning I am at the mercy
of greater forces. Meaning because joy is limited
it is infinite. From this high verandah I see cloud fronts,
the high and low of tides, shafts of sun whitening
the whitecaps, rain melding, the sea steel blue, the long day's
gloom and lightness like a pulse. And then the bee,
which is abundance, sharing solitude, alights on a rain lily.

Rain

Then the rain, gentle and endless and sour
through the brutal days. Waking to black
clouds and when I go to sleep they are still there,
still black clouds, still releasing their millions of drops
as if lethargy and exhaustion were a disease
released by alien forces and permeating the galaxy,
the hemisphere. It is a windless week
and still the city floods. The clouds descend

from nowhere then. Above. Materialise. Whatever.
The rain falls softer than spiders' webs,
and only late at night, for five minutes, at
the height of isolation, does it drum. And only
poetry matters then, snatching heat and healing
from the jaws of decay. At night there is the noise
of rain, by day the sight and sound of it. You
are somewhere else now. But the rain is always here.

Small Spaces

The long slow pink sky. The deep fact
of the trees. The green quivering of leaves
in the blue time of lilacs. The neurotic flit
of tiny birds and the swaying of the branches
where they land. Movement all day through the bars.
A hard hot world outside. Underbellies
of airplanes. The day dawdles into dusk.
At night the screech of fruitbats causing havoc

in the palms. A small fan moves the air
in here. I burn mosquito coils, sleep briefly,
move towards psychosis. Dawn. Another day
to pace. Suddenly I notice the arcing of trees
and the sky is filled with sparks. Always
there and only now seen? The world
from my window a sparkplug of series thereof.
I try to hold myself inside my own silence.

Wind

The wind blows from the south. It always does.
From out the bay, along the docks, through every boat,
it howls through gaps in every borrowed flat.
And it brings goosebumps and the tinkle and flap
of rigging. There is nowhere for the wind to go
but fluidly, through all things on the globe.
We all are skinny things. It buffets us. South
there is a lake I read about, three thousand metres

under the ice, undisturbed for a million years.
Antarctica of archetypal dreams. And what am I
plugged into? Aridity of gymnasiums, rhythms
of the dislocated days. The wind finds its level
like water. Poet as naturalist: molecules
of aluminium tumble through the window frame when
molecules of atmosphere slam into them. Atoms
of eucalypt, too: the trees bent double.

Summer

The sky broods like the whole of Sydney's
done something wrong and it can't quite put its finger
on it. Christmas stretches into New Year and
Sydneysiders wear the vacant stare of the slightly
troubled. This is nothing, you think. Humidity
of gathering crowds. Everyone heads to the beach
and the beach too is not quite right, the way
the water stalks foreigners, the way the seaweed

crunches underfoot, the way the wind whips sand
into your fillings. This is nothing, you think.
Diving onto the sandbar, the boy breaks his neck
and the helicopter takes him away. Too much sun,
everywhere. All a helicopter ever meant
is *Apocalypse Now*, the way its blades shimmer
in the salt haze. The gulls go more insane than ever,
if that's possible, and later you learn the neck boy dies.

Blood

The leaves are budding on the trees. The buds
are popping everywhere. Spring, as in spring in the step,
makes sense. In Paris there is the dead of Winter,
as in you think of death, as in great boats
of the dead ploughing through oceans of sky.
And then one week, bang, there is Spring
and it feels like Summer. You can almost hear
that popping and the blood quickens in the turtles

you're minding, in that they're slightly less spaced out
than usual. I read once that's how reptiles work.
But for us in sun the blood slows down to dream.
There's a pulse in the world you're beginning to take.
The blood too sails through the long repair.
Eyes closed in the quiet you hear both beats.
There is you, which is good, who you like, and
then the trees, ready to explode into light.

Fish

In Sydney it's always Spring and then it falls into Summer
and in Paris it's Spring today. I see a white cat
and a black crow and this means nothing, absolutely nothing,
its own kind of happiness. 'Trees tumble out of twigs
and sticks,' ed cummings said, and rightly so.
All his best poems were about Spring. In Paris
it's tumbling into tomorrow but today is better,
always, the heart of the heart of the gift. I visit

the dusty aquarium and stare at a blue fish. Means
not a thing. Not a thing but joy and a blueness
bordering on ancient. I'm lost in there. The blue fish
does nothing, repeatedly, and is beautiful. Suspends.
'Monsieur, on va fermer'—the ushers snap me out of it.
Outside, the mauve of a dusk softer than usual
blends with the mauve of petrochemical smog. We are in
the time of cars. The Parisians make their way home.

The Bridges of Paris

... Nothing forbids us from seeking a loving approach
to that which lies beyond our reach ...

—Goethe

The pale rose city of Paris at dusk in Spring.
Goethe said colours are the deeds and sufferings
of light. Overwhelmed in such a city,
guy ropes cut loose from the dock that you were,
you drift across bridges, you linger. You succumb
to the river of light, vast estuaries in flood
above the Seine streaming through your head as dusk
hardens to indigo and the dark earth barges on

and night positions itself on the contours of gargoyles.
You know nothing about anything and sense this gratefully
as the complete you. The moon issues palely forth.
Even the fish are happy, and the birds, which are fish
in the rivers of light, careering weightless into the depths.
One by one the lights come on and the stars take shape
like the luminescence of algae in the ocean of darkness
that rivers become. It's a sumptuous night.

The Lavender Minutes

Seventy-seven times—I don't exactly count but it's a nice
    number—
the bee gulps greedily from the lavender flowers he's harvesting,
and seventy-seven times the purple cups quiver and bounce
as if a single arrow of breeze were singling them out one stem
at a time. So I concentrate on the bee. I am in the realm of
one minute at a time because that's where concentrating on the
bee takes me. It's a place to bow down in. *Goulûment*
is how the bee drinks: lustily, greedily, the two words together.

You'd say: 'Je t'embrasse goulûment'—I kiss you greedily—
and the idea is drinking at the fountain of the bounteous.
One minute at a time I am in the fleeting bounty and subject
to caprices of the weather. The bee lives for a week or two
and this is where sorrow comes in: seventy-seven heartbeats
and already a minute is gone. Even as the world rolls on and time
itself devours itself the condition is voraciousness. The
    thunderstorm
arrives, broils. Enter lightning; in a flash the bee is gone.

Rue des Abbesses

And here's the thing. The sky's been there
forever and a day. The reasons for its being blue

get lost in the contemplation
of its blueness. Giselle said that would be

a form of meditation, and that you step back
from your life the better to move into it.

Is Autumn good? It's better to ask,
how could you not love Autumn? Even

as things die the sky arches over abundance
wherever you are. What the sky is

is geometry but this means many things.
Geometries then: not measurement so much as

perspective, the placing of ourselves
among all the blue and green, which is big;

which is huge and a bit; which is forever
and a day. So it's a soft geometry then

in the way that even glass is a liquid,
and it's a question of dignity in the way

that we touch each other while the windows
flow downwards and our bones decompose

in the hugeness. All this happens so slowly
it's hard to notice—not the touching,

but the melting and the crumbling.
What you get given is a moment of sun, is

always a fragment, and you let it go
as it goes through you, and you

are the fuller for being the lighter
and since every moment cannot be repeated,

ever, you are the hungrier
for having devoured it.

Excavation

—Pella, Jordan

A la fin tu es las de ce monde ancien...
—Apollinaire, 'Zone'

And all the world is biscuit-shaped
it's up to me to feed my face...
—XTC, 'Senses Working Overtime'

From Jordan I am drawn
down the funnel of the Rift
backwards through prehistory
to the rush of galaxies.

I feel a beginning tremor
at the destruction horizon
of Pella. I wind up fearing
the Heat Death of the Universe,

jetlagged at this confluence
of continents, believing
and beliefs. High on
Jabal Sartaba fossils throw

themselves at my feet
saying, 'Trilobite. Arthropod.'
My head pounds in response
to the earth's tectonic squeeze.

Storms circle the valley,
trapped for days. Then suddenly
they clear, and on Tel Husn,
watching the sun skirt the sky

as the earth curves away,
the wind screams through
my head. At eye level
hundreds of birds

ride on turbulent currents
of light through the cliffs.
On Tel Husn men as old
as trees cart dirt

and through the gnats and dust,
in tachyonic vertigo, all
is superluminal, hyperlight,
each atom a mind waiting

to recognize itself, all
the world a wave function
waiting to be popped.
Above my head a swoosh

of wind brings consciousness
of waterfalls: I look up
to a flock of birds
effortless on jetstreams

of pure momentum
over my right shoulder,
swooping to the river
far below. Gliding,

and all the world aglow.
'In the end you are tired
of that world of antiquity.'
At sunset the sun

leaves a pulse and a print
on my eye, trembling
liquid on the black
rim of earth.

The sun itself always
a print of what it was
seven lonely minutes ago
across a cold arc

through space. Bearings.
Bearings. I think of Bondi
in two directions
over two horizons

around a closed sphere.
'In the end you are tired
of this ancient world'—
because of home, the beach.

Because the beach is there.
Because the beach is always
and forever only ever
of itself; and because

it's always 6.00 p.m., long
daylight saving days,
at the end of a hot one,
hours of light to go.

Airmail

Miranda. I'm 33,000 feet over Istanbul
which is as close as I've ever been to it,
but not as close as I will be one day.
33,000 feet. Only about seven miles.
Horizontal, I'd still be in the suburbs, or on
the island you told me about, the island
in the Bosphorus Strait, and there's only
one car on the island, the mayor's car.
You told me about that. I've been wondering
if there's a mechanic shop as well, but
the more I think about it, the more
I guess not. Still, the way you told it
gets to me, and something of you is echoing
here even though I'm not in Paris now
but ten kilometres above Istanbul, straight up.
What else? Ottoman Empire architecture,
you said, where you stayed. Not being clear on this
I see something quaint and wooden and Swiss
from schoolbooks. You said horse and buggy is

the transport, and it would take an hour
to circle the island this way, so I picture you
doing that, clop clop clop, your eyes devouring light,
your skin attuned to everything. Everything.
You told me you were there
in Winter but I've only known you in Autumn
so now I picture you from a photo you showed me
(I picture you from a picture). In the photo
you are standing by an icy black road
in front of a snow-filled forest. The trees
are like black sticks and everything else
is white. The dead of Winter
in the south of France, but you're in the photo,
Miranda, so let's say it's better to say heart.
The heart of Winter. In the photo
you are beautiful, not the least because
you are, but also because of the way
it could be a black and white photo
if not for the red of your lips and the faint
blush in your cold cheeks, which is blood,
you see, expressing itself quietly. Or it could be
a colour photo, of you in front of
a giant black and white billboard that's advertising
trees or snow. Maybe it's possible
to see your blue eyes in the photo, too,

I can't remember right now.

                              So that's
how I picture you, in the carriage, in Winter,
on the island near Istanbul, a beret
and overcoat framing your bright pale face.
And then I see you taking off the beret
and the overcoat, in a cafe by the dock,
where you told me you played backgammon
with the old men by the fire. Miranda
trouncing the local champ. 'Four in a row.
I didn't backgammon him, but four's pretty good.'
Miranda drinking coffee and cranking out
the hot dice.

                    But most of all I picture you
and the morning you woke up in;
the way you told it gets to me. It's Winter
on the island near Istanbul and your room
is the attic room, the high window looking out
over the strait. The sky is clear, the kind of
cold blue I've never known myself. Bitterly
cold means there's nothing sweet about the day
so that's not a description I'd want to use here.
The wind is blowing the snow across the water.
The snow comes skittering over the surface
and, hitting the island, fans upwards. Whoosh! So

it looks to you as if it's snowing out of the water
and towards the sky! The flakes swirl
everywhere, around the island, around your window,
and you feel yourself to be in the midst
of a great wonder. The morning is awash
with a ballet of flakes; gold, they could be fireflies.
It's a muffled white beauty you've woken into,
a silence so thick in the Bosphorus morning
that your pulse fills the bedroom like a drum.
I picture you stretching and then I picture you
smiling. This is moving into the realm
of pure imagination (you didn't actually
describe such details) but what you evoked
has a momentum of its own now.
Your fingertips, pressed to the window,
feel the wind hum through the glass.
Snow everywhere. In the dry discomfort
of a long flight, I am picturing all this,
imagining Miranda who is lingering in images.
No one flake the same, they say, no
one day repeated, and aeroplanes are cylinders
for taking us away. Imagining Miranda.
Imagining Miranda of the Snows.
In airspace there's reverie, which is a form
of desire. So there's you, who I don't know

well, emerging from your own memory
to lodge a while in mine, in an image
I can't shake, and all I can say is,
thank God for small unshakeabilities.

Four Postcards

1. Earlier, the first half million years, there was nothing to see. They say: 'And God said, "Let there be light,"' but it wasn't exactly like that. They say: 'Big Bang', and we picture a fireball, a *visible* thing, expanding, but it wasn't exactly like that either. It was hot, yes. Oh Jesus, it was hot!—do you remember that? The excitation of atoms. The first few minutes in the universe it was a billion degrees. We're talking celsius. And dark. It was utterly dark. This is the 'fireball', then. You can feel it but you can't see it. A map soup of electrons and photons and black body radiation.

2. At half a million years, the temperature has dropped— diffused by space's own colossal expansion—to 3000 degrees. Now the free electrons have slowed down enough to attach themselves to nuclei. And at last, from now, the universe becomes transparent to photons. In the Beginning was the Word, and the Word was Light, but not for half a million years. And the Light rained down upon the heavens and the earth, but not for half a million years. We are pierced by photons from the depths of space.

There's the solar wind, and the way ghosts shimmer, and the tussling of your hair, in the bright sun, in the park.

3. All this was a long time before the galaxies began to swirl themselves into being. For a long time we were photons bombarded by photons. For a long time we collided. *Ils sont où, les photons fatigués?* Gone, gone forever. The visible horizon is always just beyond us. Now there's so much space that collision is merely memory. For long ages now, in the silence, we meet nobody. At four a.m. the TV turns to snow. There, in the spaces between the pixels, luminous figures begin to appear. In my delirium, of course, I mistake them for angels. I know that the observable universe is big, so I figure they've been flying for a very long time.

4. Then the visible horizon shrinks suddenly to the event horizon, inside which is hidden the black hole, and all the history of how it formed, and all its information, all its light. Ah but we felt our heart shudder at that distant implosion. Ah but we can never go there. In the black hole, for the first time in memory, visibility becomes absence. We read of 'Force 12' on the Beaufort Scale—a hurricane: *'Air filled with foam; sea completely white with driving spray; visibility greatly reduced.'* We picture

drowning sailors hallucinating Christ come to breathe His serene oxygen into their blue lips. We picture bones calcifying in the ocean's dark trenches.

Crescent Moon Over
the Eiffel Tower

First I think of Jesus, or not actually Jesus,
but the vapour trail from a jet, which makes
a line across the hard sky parallel with the top
of my window, which makes me think of Apollinaire
who said in a poem that Jesus is the holder
of the world high altitude record, a truly modern
aviator, and that's how I think of Jesus,
being in Paris and all, the thing with Apollinaire.
But I'm looking at the line the vapour trail makes,
which way up in the sky would form a perfect T
with the tip of the Eiffel Tower (the tip of the
Tour Eiffel sounds better in a poem) if the *Tour Eiffel*
were a fair whack higher. You know what I mean:
blue symmetries of summer. And *then* I notice,
and here's what the poem's about, when my eyes
are making the imaginary T, just above the point
where my imaginary much higher *Tour Eiffel*
would meet the vapour trail, a crescent moon.
A crescent moon so thin and faint it's almost not there

in the hot white Paris sky. But it is there,
and it's above the Eiffel Tower, pardon,
la Tour Eiffel, and it's above the vapour trail
that Jesus in a jet has made. What do I learn
from this experience? Well, in two weeks' time,
if the weather holds, and it should, there'll be
a fat full moon over Paris, and I'm up the hill
in Montmartre, with a view to fucking die for.
I can see three quarters of the sky, so I'm sure
that around two weeks from now, one way
or another, I'll be seeing that fat full moon.
And this is a thought that is not at all unpleasant.

Lisbon

Da Gama knew not fear. At ten we read these things
and still we became clerks.

Vasco da Gama. Yet there, back then, in the wailing
of the wave-torn seas; in the strain and the squeal

of the ropes as thick as wrists; in the sacred heart
of Christ dangling golden round our necks, Christ

Master Mariner of the Charts, Christ
believed by all of us to be the last port, Christ

the Diver who would swoop us from the mouths
of sea-beasts and kiss into our blue lips

His serene oxygen; in the gale's dark fury
and the venom of the clouds—there, back then,

at ten years old we foresaw the world this way:
the vigour of things, of the spirit and the storm.

Ourselves thrust into that fury and force.
Inundated by the onrush. Loving da Gama

as metaphor more than history. For a short while
we entered the salt-soaked air sweeping us

to the horizon; then we became clerks and I,
for one, was a clerk of the damned.

And so it is surprising to become a child again.
In Lisbon the air is awash with perfumes, orange rind

and jacaranda and a thousand swallows reel
through the bruised-plum sky. A tender city. Legend says

these are the Thousand Swallows of Lisbon and will always
be there and I, for one, today, am entered

into the heart of legend. In Lisbon's blue spring I have
myself. Blossoms fall heavy from flowers like figs

and rain down the hills of Lisbon until the sidewalks
are a carpet of petals. It's a love poem, somehow, then.

Part Two
STILL LIFE

Weather

Monday

Breathing and dreaming sustain you through despair
in the tepid atmosphere of the gnarly day:
that is what way weird and way wired mean.

Tuesday

The way you hate yourself. The world was always
dished like this, buckets of it soaking you.
Your shoulders sag like your shirts on the line.

Wednesday

A change. The weather, not your mood. It matches.
The world a fox trap snapping hard on bone,
the bright air fraught with clanging, filled with menace.

Thursday

You are as little as you could be
and out of your depth in the panic of things.
That is all you are today.

Friday

You fiddle with the dial of the shortwave of the soul.
The banshees wail on the arctic wind
and fade in the night to the hissing of space.

Saturday

The glare of distance holds your eyes. You miss
everything, a horizon you can't know, and you miss
her too. She's in Spring and you're in Autumn.

Sunday

In the blue time of lilacs, you come to know
that all weather passes. Wake up, know this,
there it is, the blue lilac weather.

The Veins of
Howard Hughes

Howard sleeps straight through,
nine and a half hours. Needed that,
and it happens every now
and again. So feeling a bit
fragile at such distance between shots
he knows nonetheless this could be
an ideal opportunity to squeeze
out a shit before the first hit
of the day. He leans out of bed,
mixes up, takes the syringe with him
to the bathroom, just to know
it's there. Howard settles into this
exhausting inconvenience to the routines
of inertia. Howard says aloud,
'This will not take long'—attempt
to believe more than statement
of fact. He reads *Aviation Weekly*
but the pick sits on the basin sharper

than anything else in the bathroom.
So he picks it up to read
its calibrations, which are holy
in an oddly medicinal way.
He taps an air bubble to the top
of the barrel. All this microscopic
activity puts the tang of comfort
in the back of Howard's throat, so
it is impossible to concentrate on shitting
any more. 'Maybe tomorrow,' Howard thinks.
'Maybe tomorrow I'll shit it all out.'

Premonition of Her Disappearance from the Life

You were driving, already a driving downwards.
I woke from deep sleep on a grey morning
to stare at the white lines rushing by.
To each side poles and poplars in a blur.

I think the birds half asleep in the drizzle
whispered to us their consternation. Already
you'd become hemmed in by pulses not your own.
Oh Morgan, the unfairness of electricity!

We were miles and miles from Five Mile Beach
where a shack stood still as time could not
on the cold white sands:
the kiosk of the provisions of your heart,

boarded up for winter or forever.

Miscarriage

Her heaving stomach now
is summer cool.

Contraction without end
diminishes.

The stillest birth. It was
no more than that,

in the cold theatre,
under the monstrous

shadows of nurses,
in the pungent atmosphere.

The pethidine, the pain,
I imagine, for her,

gave lie to the meaningless
idea of order,

and through her blinding tears
she said to me,

'I hear the bull stamp
at the gate of decay,

the stupid red bull smashing
posts in the pen of despair.

And yet I hope my heart is not
this stony heart of death.'

History of Violence

In the landscape
the flesh &

when the flesh is gone
the landscape

In the rocks
history's throbbing &

beyond us, beneath us, the mute
seams of desire

In the rain
the erasure &

in the wind pillars
and pillars of salt—

scattering of memory,
descent of the burden

of consciousness.
The rocks love not God

but the earth heaves
in His breast,

its crust His
bloodied breastplate ...

God remembers nothing
ever

—cannot afford to
does not want to—

thus stays sane

Childhood Terror

At Minnamurra Avenue. The bush.
The creek. My father and I.
We went to the edge of the falls for revenge,
to find my attacker the magpie.

The afternoon grey, the black bird gone,
my sobbing subsiding. Dad held my hand,
hurled rocks into the empty trees, screamed
at the black bush, 'Go away!'
I loved him for pretending.

Bodies of Water

1. From Swimming Pool to Ocean

In that time and in those days
domestic cats will swim in pools
and magpies saunter cockily
across the lawn and bully them.
You will not know which animals
are friend or foe. The magpies will
loom taller than bedraggled cats.
The yard will shrink, the sky will drop.
From deep pelagic dreams you will
awake with phrases ready-formed
and learn from messages of sleep,
from that of you which can decode
the way of you. Its clarity
your clarity, the voice of God
the voice within. To know to act;
and how to hack into the world
the path of the immediate,
and see the light inside the light,
the structure of the visible.

The huge waves moan. The spray explodes
aloof and senseless on the rocks.

2. Death by Drowning

You see the body gentle in
the sea's enormous to and fro
uncertain as to sea or shore.
Fat lady in an overcoat,
unreal and waterlogged expanse
investigated by a gull
between each rush of salt and foam.
Police in wetsuits on the shore
are focusing binoculars.

She is not you, for now at least.
The words appear in front of you:

> *the sad thing is that*
> *she hath inherited*
> *order without kingdom*
> *merit without grace*

The Persistence of Loss

The leaves are budding on the trees.
Karen is not here today
and won't be again.
Half of what you think you are

is half of you not there
and it's hard in Spring.
Ice cracks in far Alps
and yearns for the Seine and will have it

soon. Karen is not here today.
Summer is coming in or so
the early daffodils believe.
A long Spring yet.

She's not here nor will she be.

History of Real Estate

Christians!—and the gleaming hydraulic palisades
of expansion. Centuries, millennia
of the best hill in town, in the name
of the father and always something bigger
and some holy shit or other.
God's wrath an arrow desiring
to be drunk with the blood of your heart.
In the wilderness, remember this.
But not for long. The embers of actions
long since scattered. The harnessing
of demons was our task. The clearing
of the forests the result. Conifer, eucalypt,
rain. You name it. We built cathedrals
to house Plato's peripherals. All that
head stuff. We missed the motherboard,
where it always was, in the gut.

Prayer in May

God relieve the dark unease
God of valves untie my throat
God let sink the weight of mind
to the belly of the heart's content

From Theory to Pulse

—Church of St Etienne du Mont, Paris

ecause that force through green fuse drives all flowers
vhich we would call the greater force, or God, or minor gods)
ld gathers in a place like this—things gather, here and there—
.en it's a good place to come to sit a while, though
.e first postulate of relativity, and I believe it, says to me
.ere's no such thing as place. But here I am. It's nice to sit a while.
rotect me, then, in the gathering up, in the going away.
he gargoyles do the warding off, the message gets projected
rough the spires. That's the theory. Sounds beautiful
 me. Okay. So you know nothing about anything
:cept what you recognise as instance, as kindred appearance.
iffering, then. And then compassion. There are older agonies
an churches. You go home exhausted in the middle of the day.
inlight floods the apartment. The turtle dozes by the window,
ore solemn than a thousand cats. You lie down,
ace her on your chest. For two hours she stares at you
id feels your heart move her shell. Older agonies.
)u are as little as you could be. Protect me—why?

No need. The turtle, mute, knows nothing too. That force
that through your black heart pumps conjoins the turtle here.
Of her own will she is still and yet at eighty-four beats per minute
you watch her body make that tiny jolt ten thousand and eighty time
We'll all be dead. And very soon. And yet unblackening is relief.
The diamond glint in the ancient eye. Small suffering joins
with the greater that of the ages of blood. Agonies of evolution
and beyond that, as always, geology. The lilac knows nothing of this.

Notes

'Dew' (page 3): 'Foxground'—on the New South Wales south coast, in the Kangaroo Valley.

'Sea Shanty II' (page 17): 'Beware of the Chathams!'—a 19th Century sailor's warning, originally referring to Chatham Island and outlying rocks, the only land between New Zealand and Cape Horn; later a more general warning to beware of shoals. This poem contains several other examples of 19th and 20th Century naval slang.

'Pollen' (page 23): 'The unified field'—in particle physics, unified field theory is the attempt, as yet unsuccessful—even Einstein gave up on it—to construct a theoretical framework in which electromagnetism (events at the quantum level) and gravity (large-scale events) would emerge as different aspects of a single fundamental field. 'Wave is amplified and particle is amplified'— in 1905 Einstein showed that light, which had been thought of as a wave, must also be seen as being particle-like, localised in discrete packets called photons. In physics, the 'wave-particle duality' is the notion arising from this: that light and other physical entities, such as electrons, possess both wave-like and particle-like characteristics.

'Flowers' (page 31): 'the solar wind'—technically speaking, the solar wind is a flux of particles ejected from the outer regions of the Sun at velocities great enough to escape the Sun's gravitational field, and creating detectable shock-waves on collision with the earth's magnetic field.

'Ezekiel' (page 35): 'Open the pod bay door, HAL.'—unsuccessful order given by Dave (Keir Dullea), trying to gain re-entry to the main space-ship, to HAL the computer, in Kubrick's *2001: A Space Odyssey*.

'Rue des Abbesses' (page 53): 'in the way that even glass is a liquid'—or, more properly, an 'amorphous solid', which behaves in ways similar to liquids, albeit more slowly. This is why very old glass 'pools' towards the bottom of window panes. 'The atomic or molecular structure of glasses is similar to that of the liquids from which they come. [But] whereas liquid is characterized by rapid motions of individual molecules, these motions are much smaller in glass.' (*Encyclopedia Britannica*.)

'Excavation' (page 55): 'the destruction horizon of Pella'—in archaeology, the destruction horizon is the material contained within a destruction that occurred across the site as a whole; as such it would represent a 'slice' of the life of the site at the time of the catastrophe. At Pella, the demise of the Bronze Age city in 1150 BC can clearly be seen in the destruction horizon running through some trenches, a thick black line of compressed charcoal and soot. It is not clear whether this destruction was due to war or earthquake. 'the Heat Death of the Universe'—one of two possible theories regarding the fate of the universe. The other involves the notion of the 'Big Crunch': if the gravitational attraction of all the matter in the universe is strong enough, then the universe will eventually stop expanding, and go into reverse. 'What about the other case, when there isn't enough gravitating stuff to halt the expansion? Our universe would then have time to run down to a final heat death... If our universe expands forever, there *will* be enough time for all stars, all galaxies, to attain a terminal equilibrium... eventually the atoms will themselves decay

...given enough time, white dwarfs and neutron stars would dissolve away; so would any diffuse intergalactic gas...so immensely dilute does everything become that there would eventually, on average, be less than one electron in a volume as large as our present observable universe.' (Martin Rees, *Before the Beginning: Our Universe and Others.*)

'Crescent Moon Over the Eiffel Tower' (page 69): 'Apollinaire/who said in a poem that Jesus is the holder/of the world high altitude record'—from the poem 'Zone' in *Alcools* (1913): 'C'est le Christ qui monte au ciel mieux que les aviateurs/Il détient le record du monde pour la hauteur'.

'Lisbon' (page 71): Vasco da Gama (c.1460–1524), Portuguese navigator whose voyages opened up the sea routes from western Europe to the East via the Cape of Good Hope.

Acknowledgements

Thanks to Peter Porter for taking the time and the trouble to comment on many aspects of this manuscript as it took shape, and to my editor, Andrew Wilkins, whose help on matters both creative and technical was invaluable. My gratitude to the Literature Fund of the Australia Council for making breathing space possible. Heartfelt thanks to Bernard and Mary Loughlin, Grainne Millar and all other staff at the Tyrone Guthrie Centre for the Arts at Annaghmakerrig, County Monaghan, Ireland, an extraordinary environment in which to complete this book. Thanks to Christa Munns, Edwina Johnson and all the other staff at Allen & Unwin. And huge thanks to Sophie Cunningham, my publisher and friend, for agreeing that 'Poetry redeems from decay the visitations of the divine in Man', and for publishing this book in a climate where poetry means risk.

Some of these poems have already appeared in *Heat*, *Meanjin*, *Southerly*, *RePublica*, *Ulitarra* and *Let Dark Memory Bloom*.

The author and publishers would like to thank the following for permission to reproduce copyright material: The line from 'Le Monocle de Mon Oncle' in the poem 'Passage of Time' (page 11) taken from *Opus Posthumous* by Wallace Stevens. Reprinted by permission of Faber & Faber Ltd. 'I'm A Believer' in the poem 'Safety of Descent' (page 29) words and music by Neil Diamond © 1966 Stonebridge Music and Foray Music (75%). Used by permission of Music Sales Ltd. All rights reserved. International copyright secured. © 1966 Screen Gems–EMI Music Inc. (25%). Used by permission. All rights reserved. The line from 'darling!

Printed in Great Britain
by Amazon

87385042R00072